See Me For Me

By : Dana Geall

Illustrated by : Nugraha

See Me for Me is inspired by triplets, Taylor, Cole, and Brody, who were born prematurely, and as a result have cerebral palsy. All three children use wheelchairs and live full and happy lives. Although the children face tremendous challenges, they share a positive attitude and great personalities. Taylor, Cole, and Brody teach us every day to look beyond our differences and see people for who they truly are.

This book is dedicated to my children for always inspiring everything that I do. I love you.
—Mom

Everyone is different.
Each person is unique.
Try not to judge another
for how they look or speak.

Be open, kind, and friendly,
equity should be your aim.
We're all in this together,
even though we're not the same.

You'll meet a lot of people,
who are different than you.
Take the time to know them,
and to learn their point of view.

Now, here are three amazing kids
who stand out in a crowd.
They're full of personality
and make us very proud.

Here's Taylor in her wheelchair.
She rolls from place to place.
She'll take on any challenge
with a smile upon her face.

She's quite a funky dancer,
and she sings and acts for fun.
When people say she can't or won't,
she shows them how it's done.

Her brother Cole's a gamer.
He's hooked, as you can see.
He wants to be a programmer.
He loves technology.

He wears cochlear implants.
They're made to help him hear.
It is such a gift to listen to
the ones he holds most dear.

Young Brody is a swimmer.
Every day his dearest wish
is to leave his wheelchair by the pool
and swim just like a fish.

He's a wizard in the classroom,
though his voice isn't heard.
He communicates in other ways,
and understands each word.

When you really look at people
for who they truly are.
You'll see they've overcome a lot,
and each one is a star!

If you meet somebody different,
you might accidentally stare.
Instead, say, "Hi!" and, "How are you?"
Let friendship grow from there.

Though we don’t all look familiar,
if you delve beneath the skin,
you may stumble on a heart of gold
that’s beating there within.

Put yourself in their shoes,
every triumph, every strife.
It makes us feel inspired
as we journey on through life.

Look past our outer differences
to see personality.
Embrace uniqueness and potential —
Diversability.

Make a change to help each other,
and use your strongest voice
to speak up for the ones who can't.
We all can make that choice.

EQUAL
RIGHTS

Like asking that our buildings
are accessible to all,
from the classroom to the movies,
from the restaurant to the mall.

There are many kinds of people,
north and south and east and west.
It's something we should celebrate.
Diversity's the best.

Taylor, Cole, and Brody know
they're awesome as can be.
So, hear their message loud and clear,
Please just...

See Me For Me

Please Visit:

SeeMe
For Me.ca

Made in the USA
Middletown, DE
22 February 2022

61672746R00027